SPOTLIGHT ON LITERACY

Authors, Consultants, and Reviewers

MULTICULTURAL AND EDUCATIONAL CONSULTANTS

Alma Flor Ada, Yvonne Beamer, Joyce Buckner, Helen Gillotte, Cheryl Hudson, Narcita Medina, Lorraine Monroe, James R. Murphy, Sylvia Peña, Joseph B. Rubin, Ramon Santiago, Cliff Trafzer, Hai Tran, Esther Lee Yao

LITERATURE CONSULTANTS

Ashley Bryan, Joan I. Glazer, Paul Janeczko, Margaret H. Lippert

INTERNATIONAL CONSULTANTS

Edward B. Adams, Barbara Johnson, Raymond L. Marshall

MUSIC AND AUDIO CONSULTANTS

John Farrell, Marilyn C. Davidson, Vincent Lawrence, Sarah Pirtle, Susan R. Synder, Rick and Deborah Witkowski, Eastern Sky Media Services, Inc.

TEACHER REVIEWERS

Terry Baker, Jane Bauer, James Bedi, Nora Bickel, Vernell Bowen, Donald Cason, Jean Chaney, Carolyn Clark, Alan Cox, Kathryn DesCarpentrie, Carol L. Ellis, Roberta Gale, Brenda Huffman, Erma Inscore, Sharon Kidwell, Elizabeth Love, Isabel Marcus, Elaine McCraney, Michelle Moraros, Earlene Parr, Dr. Richard Potts, Jeanette Pulliam, Michael Rubin, Henrietta Sakamaki, Kathleen Cultron Sanders, Belinda Snow, Dr. Jayne Steubing, Margaret Mary Sulentic, Barbara Tate, Seretta Vincent, Willard Waite, Barbara Wilson, Veronica York

Macmillan/McGraw-Hill

A Division of The McGraw-Hill Companies

McGraw-Hill School Division
Two Penn Plaza
New York, New York 10121
Printed in the United States of America

ISBN 0-02-185877-2 / 1, L. 5

  2 3 4 5 6 7 8 9 027 03 02 01 00 99

Spotlight on Literacy

AUTHORS

ELAINE MEI AOKI • VIRGINIA ARNOLD • JAMES FLOOD • JAMES V. HOFFMAN • DIANE LAPP

MIRIAM MARTINEZ • ANNEMARIE SULLIVAN PALINCSAR • MICHAEL PRIESTLEY • CARL B. SMITH

WILLIAM H. TEALE • JOSEFINA VILLAMIL TINAJERO • ARNOLD W. WEBB • KAREN D. WOOD

Macmillan McGraw-Hill

NEW YORK • FARMINGTON

Unit 1

LET'S PRETEND

4

Unit 2

True-Blue
Friends

6

7

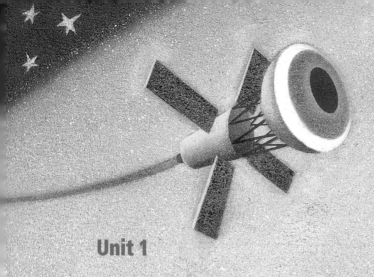

LeT'S PrEtEnd

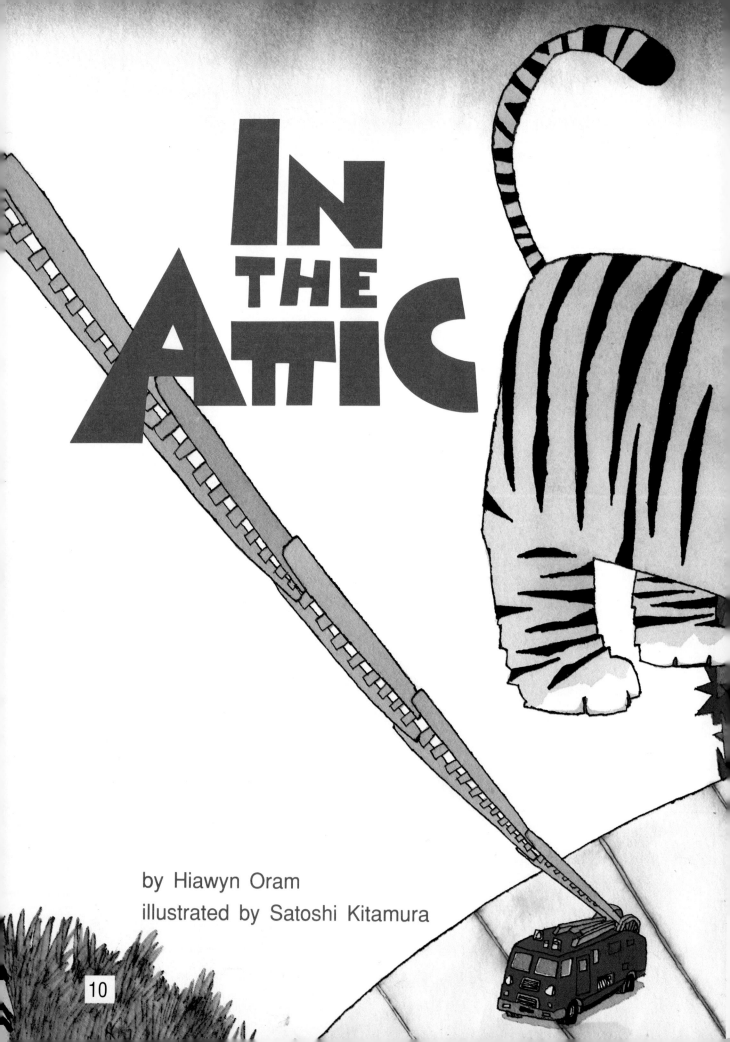

In the Attic

by Hiawyn Oram

illustrated by Satoshi Kitamura

10

I had a million toys, but I was bored.

13

So I climbed into the attic.

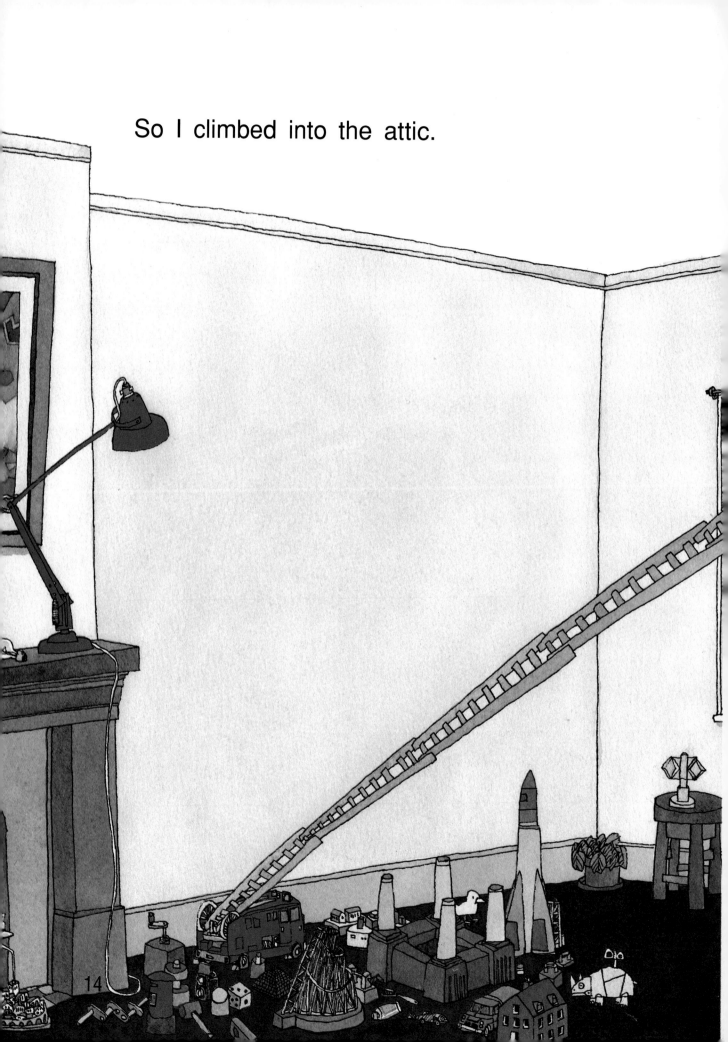

14

The attic was empty.

Or was it?

I found a family of mice . . .

. . . and a cool, quiet place to rest and think.

I met a spider and we made a web.

I opened windows to other worlds.

I found an old flying machine

and I made it work.

I went out to look for someone

to share what I had found . . .

. . . and I found a friend I could talk to.

My friend and I found a game that could

go on forever, but it was time for dinner.

So I climbed out of the attic, and
told my mother where I'd been all day.

"But we don't have an attic,"
she said.

I guess she doesn't know
about the attic.

She hasn't found the ladder.

MEET HIAWYN ORAM

Hiawyn Oram grew up in South Africa. She says, "We had no TV. All the best games I played were games of make-believe. I played them alone or with my friends. We pretended we could do anything." She adds, "*In the Attic* is about the wonderful things we make up in our minds."

MEET SATOSHI KITAMURA

Satoshi Kitamura says his idea for *In the Attic* has a hidden joke in it. "The attic is the place at the top of the house where you

put all the things you don't use. The brain is the place at the top of your head where you put ideas you don't always use! So I imagined a boy going into his attic and, using his imagination, finding all kinds of things."

SQUARE AS A HOUSE

If you could be small

Would you be a mouse

Or a mouse's child

Or a mouse's house

Or a mouse's house's

Front door key?

Who would you

Which would you

What would you be?

Karla Kuskin

Meet
Carlos Pellicer López

Carlos Pellicer López was born in Mexico in 1948. As he grew up, he studied painting. He became a very good artist. Many of his paintings were shown in art shows. One day Mr. Carlos Pellicer López began to write stories to go with his pictures. Today boys and girls can read his books in Spanish and English. His books have won many awards in Mexico.

Julieta
and Her
Paintbox

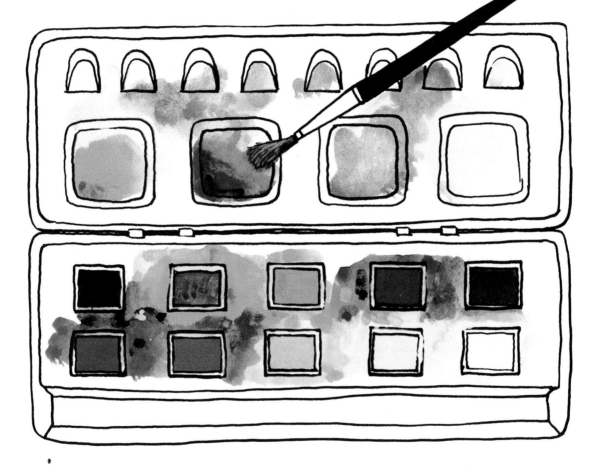

A Story Illustrated by
Carlos Pellicer López

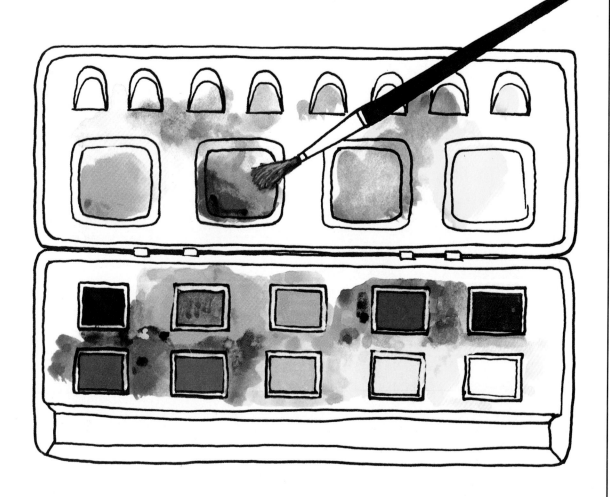

Primer Premio Antoniorrobles 1983
for best text and illustration

Julieta and Her Paintbox

For Julia and María, who fill my paintbox with color.

When they gave Julieta
a paintbox, she didn't
know how much fun it
would be.

One rainy afternoon

she couldn't go out to play with her friends. She didn't want to get bored. So she took out her paintbox and some paper. She began to paint.

She painted a city in
a distant land. It looked
like a checkerboard. It
was made of little
colored squares.

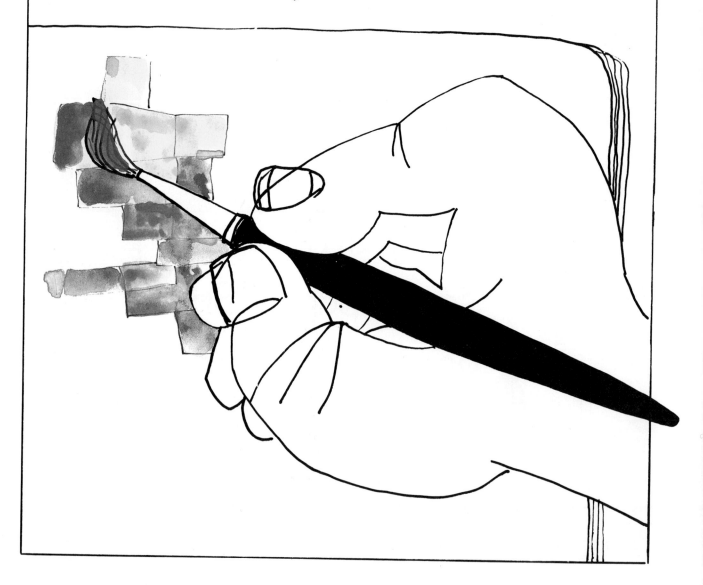

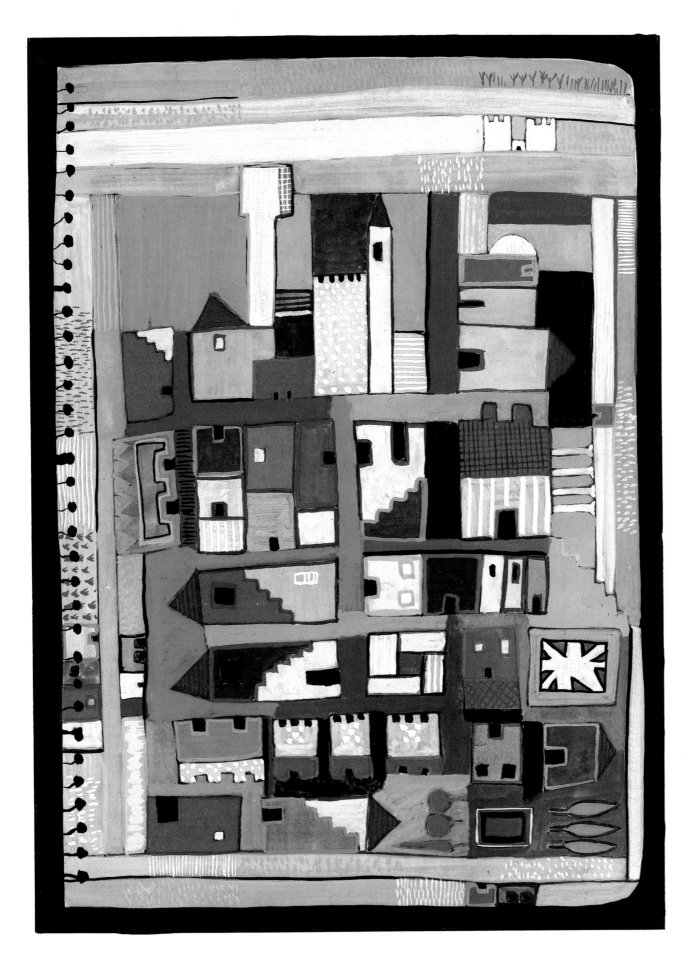

49

The next day the sun
was shining. But she
wanted to remember
that rainy afternoon.

Little by little her
paper began to fill up
with clouds and raindrops.
Finally, she saw a
big storm.

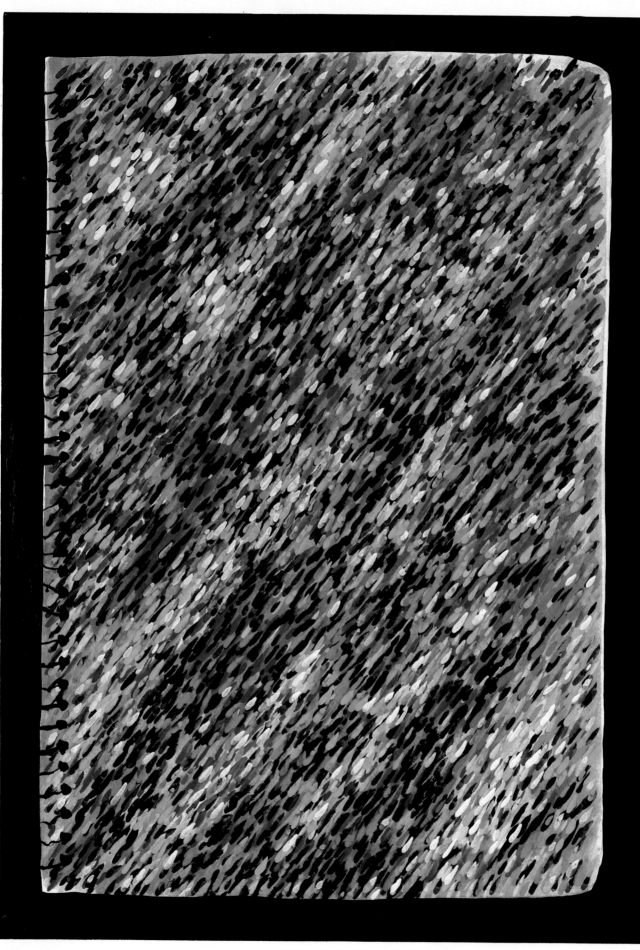

52

Julieta was having a great time. She could see on paper what she couldn't see before her eyes.

She imagined a very big strawberry. It was so big it didn't fit on the page. It was juicy, sweet, and very red.

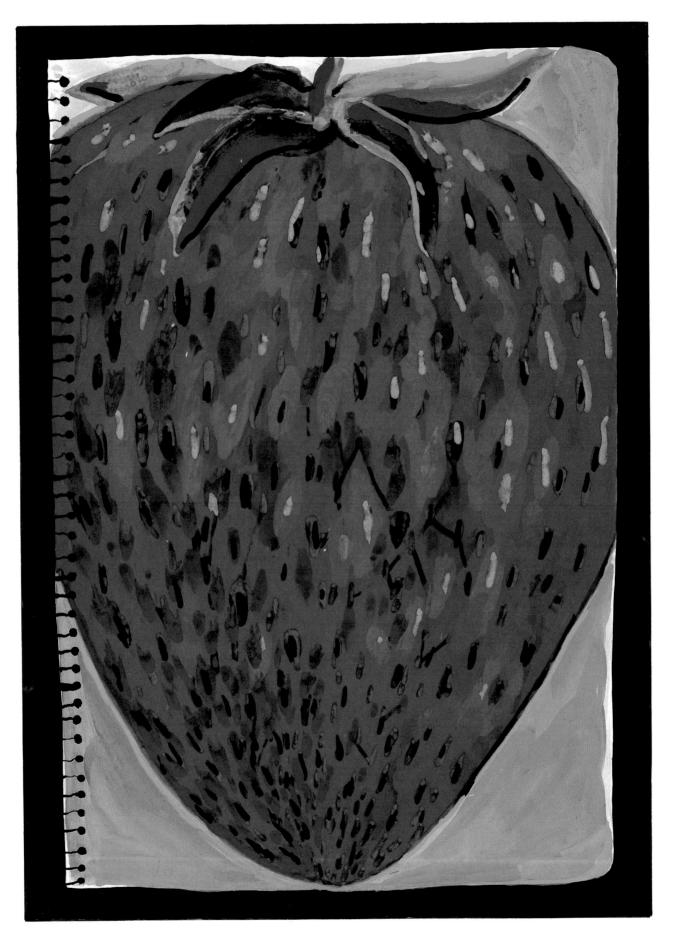

When she painted
a green donkey,
she laughed and
laughed. How
funny it looked!

And even though she
knew that donkeys weren't
green, with her paintbox
they could be.

One day she got up
early to go
to school. She
heard a lot of
birds singing
outside her
window.

All day long she kept thinking, "What is the color of birds singing?"

Before she went
to sleep, she
used her paintbox
to imagine what
she had heard
that morning.
And this is
what appeared:

That night Julieta had
strange dreams, stranger
than she had ever had before.

She was flying through the sea. All the birds and the fish and the flowers looked alike. It was such a beautiful dream! When she woke up, she was sad to see it end.

But that afternoon when she got home from school, she wanted to remember it. So she took out her favorite toy: her paintbox!

By then Julieta knew that her paintbox was magic.

Just like magicians who
pull rabbits out of hats

or make cards appear
out of thin air,

she could use her paints to make cities, rainstorms, and fruit. She could also make colored donkeys, birds' songs, and dreams appear out of the pages.

When
you know
how to
paint,
you can
say
anything.

Imaginary

by Ann Klein

Let yourself pretend to be
Creatures great and small with me.
In our imaginary zoo
We'll stretch our minds and bodies, too.

To be a goat, what you must know
Is how to prance both to and fro.
You lift your feet through paths of stone,
With head held high, all on your own!

You can be a crocodile:
Slide into the pond awhile.
Chomp your teeth and lash your tail.
Snap at froggies in your trail.

Zoo

What kind of lion would you be?
Would you snooze up in a tree?
Would you purr or would you roar
When you stretched out upon the floor?

And when you are a tall giraffe,
You can make your family laugh.
Gallop to the nearest tree
And pick a leaf most gingerly.

Like a Summer Bird

How would it be
to fly and fly
like a summer bird
in the rain-washed sky
after the sun
had ironed it dry?

How would it be
to sleep in a tree
on a rocking-chair branch
when the wind blew free,
with a sound in your ears
like the sound of the sea?

How would it *be?*

Aileen Fisher

Pat Cummings

Pat Cummings laughs when she tells why she wrote *Jimmy Lee Did It*. "When I was growing up, if something in our house got broken or disappeared, my younger brother Artie always blamed it on someone named Jimmy Lee. I never saw Jimmy Lee or heard Jimmy Lee, so I thought writing this book might be a good way to get back at Artie. I thought it would be a good joke."

Jimmy Lee Did It

By Pat Cummings

Jimmy Lee is back again
And nothing is the same.

He's causing lots of trouble,
While my brother takes the blame.

Artie made his bed, he said.
But Jimmy thinks he's smart.

While Artie read his comics,
Jimmy pulled the sheets apart.

Dad fixed us pancakes
And Artie said his tasted fine,

But Jimmy Lee had just been there
And eaten most of mine.

I heard the crash of breaking glass,
But turned too late, I guess.

"Jimmy Lee did it," Artie said,
As we cleaned up the mess.

When Artie's room got painted,
Jimmy Lee was in the hall.

He used up Artie's crayons
Drawing pictures on the wall.

And when I finally found my bear,
I asked Artie, "Who hid it?"

He told me frankly, "Angel,
It was Jimmy Lee who did it."

He caused so much trouble
That I began to see—

The only way to stop it
Was to capture Jimmy Lee.

I knew about his sweet tooth,
So I set a tasty trap,

But Jimmy Lee just waited
Till I had to take my nap.

I spread out all my marbles
To trip up Jimmy Lee.

The dog slid by and scratched the floor
And Mom got mad at me.

I hid in the hall closet
And I never made a sound,

But Jimmy Lee will only come
When Artie is around.

I don't know what he looks like,
He never leaves a trace—

Except for spills and tears
And Artie's things about the place.

Since Artie won't describe him,
He remains a mystery.

But if you're smart, you'll listen
And watch out for Jimmy Lee.

PRETENDING

When you are in bed and it's cold outside,

do you ever pretend that you have to hide?

Do you curl up your toes?

Do you wrinkle your nose?

Do you make yourself little so none of you shows?

Do you pull the sheets over the whole of your face

and pretend you are in some faraway place?

Mother thinks you are sleeping,

but she does not know

that all tucked in your bed, you have places to go.

Bobbi Katz

Meet **Johanna Hurwitz**

When Johanna Hurwitz was ten, she wanted to work in a library. But her first love was always writing. Today she has written many books for children. Some of them are funny. "Even my cats and their fleas have made it into a book," Ms. Hurwitz says.

Meet **Jerry Pinkney**

As a young boy, Jerry Pinkney liked to draw. Some of his books are about African Americans. Mr. Pinkney has also worked on books about Hispanics and Native Americans. Many of his books have won awards.

New Shoes for Silvia

written by Johanna Hurwitz
illustrated by Jerry Pinkney

Once, far away in another America, a package arrived at the post office. The package came from Tía Rosita. Inside there were gifts for the whole family.

For Silvia there was a wonderful present—a pair of
bright red shoes with little buckles that shone in
the sun like silver.

Right away, Silvia took off her old shoes and put on
the beautiful new ones. Then she walked around so
everyone could see.

"*Mira, mira,*" she called. "Look, look."

"Those shoes are as red as the setting sun," her grandmother said. "But they are too big for you."

"Your shoes are as red as the inside of a watermelon," said Papa. "But they are too big. You will fall if you wear them."

"Tía Rosita has sent you shoes the color of a rose," said Mama. "We will put them away until they fit you."

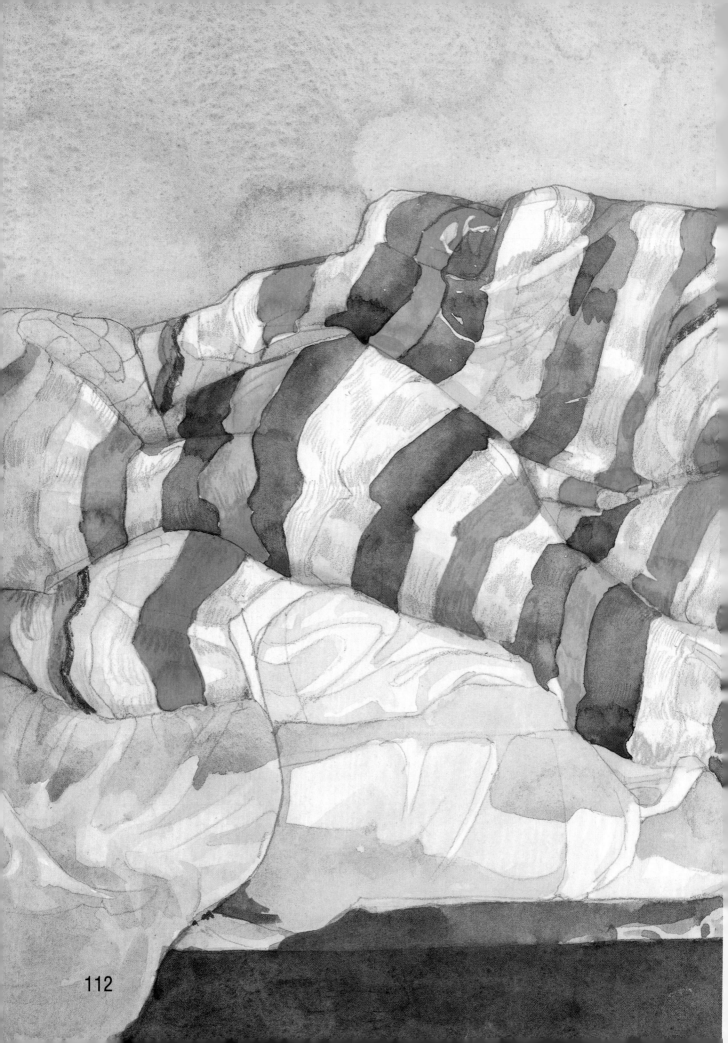

Silvia was sad. What good were new shoes if she couldn't wear them?

That night she slept with them in her bed.

The next morning Silvia put on the red shoes again. Perhaps she had grown during the night.

No. The shoes were still too big. But she saw that they were just the right size to make beds for two of her dolls. Even though it was morning, the dolls went right to sleep in their new red beds.

A week passed, and Silvia tried on the red shoes again. Perhaps she had grown during the week.

No. The shoes were still too big. But she saw that they made a fine two-car train. She pushed them all around the floor. What a good ride the babies had in their red train!

117

Another week passed, and Silvia tried on the red
shoes again. Certainly by now she had grown big
enough so they would fit.

No. The shoes were still too big. But Silvia found
some string and tied it to the shoes. Then she
pulled the shoes like oxen working in the field.

Still another week passed, and Silvia tried on the red shoes again. Would they fit now?

No. The shoes were still too big. But she saw that they were just the right size to hold the pretty shells and smooth pebbles that she had collected when she went to the beach with her grandparents.

Another week passed, and another and another. Sometimes Silvia was so busy playing with the other children or helping her mama with the

new baby or feeding the chickens or looking for their eggs that she forgot to try on her new red shoes.

124

One day Mama wrote a letter to Tía Rosita. Silvia thought about the red shoes. She emptied out all the shells and pebbles and dusted the shoes off on her skirt. They were as red and beautiful as ever. Would they fit today?

Yes.

"*Mira, mira,*" she cried, running to show Mama and the baby. "Look, look. My shoes are not too big now."

Silvia wore her new red shoes when she walked to the post office with Mama to mail the letter.

"Maybe there will be a new package for us," said Silvia.

"Packages don't come every day," said Mama.

"Maybe next time Tía Rosita will send me new blue shoes," said Silvia.

They mailed the letter and walked home. Silvia's shoes were as red as the setting sun. They were as red as the inside of a watermelon. They were as red as a rose. The buckles shone in the sun like silver.

And best of all, the shoes were just the right size for Silvia.

BOOK REVIEWS

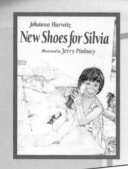

Title: **New Shoes for Silvia**
Author: Johanna Hurwitz
Illustrator: Jerry Pinkney

Reviewed by:
Maia Kallen

I liked this book very much.
I liked the games that Silvia played with her shoes. It was fun to read the part when Silvia slept with her shoes.

The pictures in the story were great! I wondered what the blue shoes would look like. It would be great if the author wrote a book about blue shoes.

This story reminded me of when I ride my bike and I pretend that it's an airplane.

B.J. Harrison

I liked this book because the little girl gets a package with a pair of new red shoes. One of my favorite parts was when Silvia tries the shoes on and they fit her! I also liked it when Silvia's mama said the shoes are as red as a rose and Silvia's papa said the shoes are as red as the inside of a watermelon.

Sometimes I use my imagination in my house. I imagine that a swivel chair is a tea cup ride on the carousel!

BJ Harrison

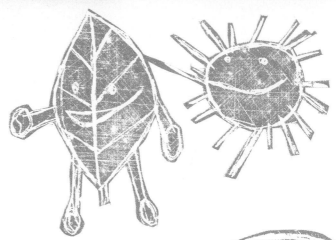

By Myself

When I'm by myself

And I close my eyes

I'm a twin

I'm a dimple in a chin

I'm a room full of toys

I'm a squeaky noise

I'm a gospel song

I'm a gong

I'm a leaf turning red

I'm a loaf of brown bread

I'm a whatever I want to be

An anything I care to be

And when I open my eyes

What I care to be

Is me

Eloise Greenfield
Illustrated by Leo and Diane Dillon

Unit 2

True-Blue Friends

Meet Ann Tompert

Ann Tompert has always loved books. As a young girl she found books fun. She says, ". . . books were the most important things in my life."

Today Ann Tompert is the author of many children's books. She also writes for children's magazines. When Ms. Tompert is not writing or reading, she likes to garden or sew.

Meet Lynn Munsinger

Lynn Munsinger has always liked to draw. Over the years she has drawn pictures for many children's books. She has also drawn pictures for greeting cards and magazines.

Ms. Munsinger likes to work with pen and ink. But she likes to work in color the most. Lynn Munsinger enjoys drawing funny animal characters. She tries to make her pictures tell a story.

JUST
A
LITTLE
BIT

Written by
Ann Tompert

Illustrated by
Lynn Munsinger

Elephant and Mouse were in the park, playing on the slides and swings. Elephant said, "Let's try the seesaw."

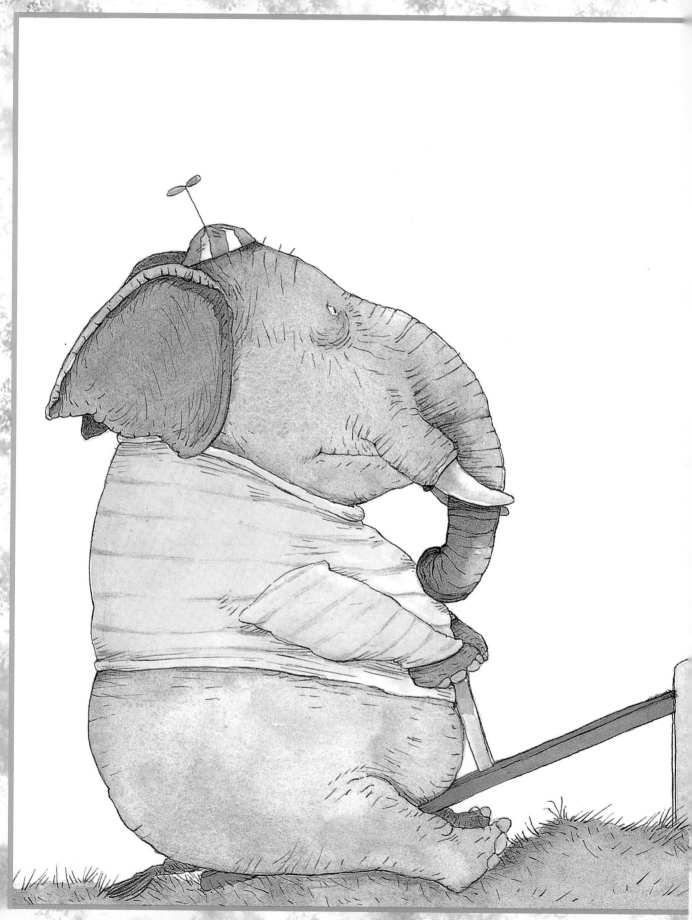

Elephant sat on the down side of the seesaw.
Mouse climbed to the very edge of the up side.
But nothing happened.

"Push down," urged Elephant. "Push down."

Mouse pushed down against the board as hard
as he could. Still, nothing happened.

Along came Giraffe. "Let me help you," she said.

Giraffe walked up the board and sat next to Mouse. Nothing happened. Elephant's end of the seesaw stayed on the ground. Mouse's end stayed in the air.

"You need just a little bit more help," said Zebra,
trotting up the seesaw.
And—nothing happened.

Elephant still stayed on the ground. Mouse still
stayed in the air.

"You need just a little bit more help," said Lion,
and he pranced up the seesaw.
And—nothing happened.

"Everyone together now," urged Elephant.
"Push down!"

Mouse, Giraffe, Zebra, and Lion pushed down
with all their might.

And—nothing happened.

By then a crowd had gathered to watch.

"I need just a little bit more help," Elephant
called out to them.

"Let me see what I can do," said Bear. As he lumbered up the seesaw toward them, Mouse, Giraffe, Zebra, and Lion grunted and groaned and grimaced as they pressed down on the board with every last bit of their strength.

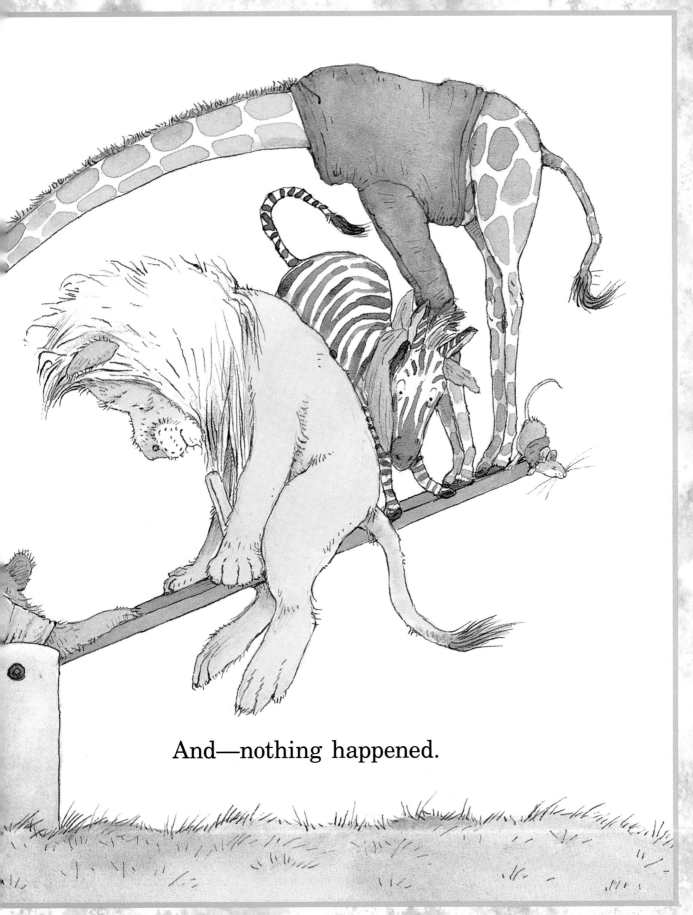

And—nothing happened.

"Oh, no," moaned the crowd.

"Who will help me just a little bit more?" Elephant called out to the crowd.

"How about me?" cried Crocodile.

"And me?" said Mongoose.

"I'll join the party," called Monkey from the banana tree overhead. She swung down onto Ostrich's back.

Crocodile, Mongoose, Monkey, and Ostrich climbed
onto the seesaw, one at a time.
And—nothing happened.

"Oh, no," moaned the crowd again.

"He'll never get off the ground," said someone in the crowd.

"Push down! Push down!" urged Elephant.

Mouse, Giraffe, Zebra, Lion, Bear, Crocodile, Mongoose, Monkey, and Ostrich grunted and groaned and grimaced as they all pushed down on the board as hard as they could.

And—nothing happened.

"They'll never do it," said someone in the crowd. "Let's go!"

The onlookers had started to move away when a small brown beetle flew down from the sky. For a moment it hovered above the seesaw. Then it flew straight to Mouse and landed on his head.

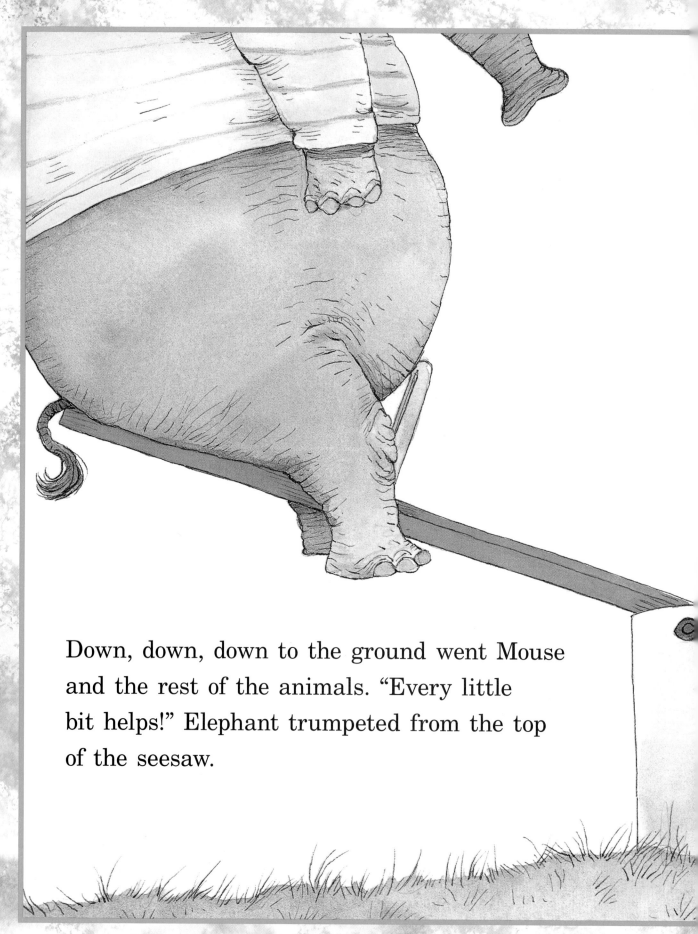

Down, down, down to the ground went Mouse
and the rest of the animals. "Every little
bit helps!" Elephant trumpeted from the top
of the seesaw.

"Hurray! Hurray! Hurray!" cheered the crowd.

With Elephant on one side and Mouse, Giraffe, Zebra, Lion, Bear, Crocodile, Mongoose, Monkey, Ostrich, and the small brown beetle on the other, they all went up and down, up and down, while the crowd cheered and clapped.

HUG O' WAR

I will not play at tug o' war.

I'd rather play at hug o' war,

Where everyone hugs

Instead of tugs,

Where everyone giggles

And rolls on the rug,

Where everyone kisses,

And everyone grins,

And everyone cuddles,

And everyone wins.

Shel Silverstein

MEET PAT MORA

Pat Mora says that children sometimes wonder why some of the words in her stories are Spanish. She tells them, "I want children reading my stories to hear the sounds they would really hear in a Hispanic home. If you came to my house, you would hear my family talking in two kinds of words—English words and Spanish words. The words have different sounds."

She adds, "All homes are alike in some ways, and different in other ways. In *A Birthday Basket for Tía*, one thing that makes Cecilia's home special is that her family speaks two languages. What are some things that make *your* home special?"

A BIRTHDAY BASKET FOR TIA

BY PAT MORA

ILLUSTRATED BY CECILY LANG

Today is secret day. I curl my cat into my arms
and say, "Ssshh, Chica. Today is secret day. Can
you keep our secret, silly cat?"

Today is a special day. Today is my great-aunt's ninetieth birthday. Ten, twenty, thirty, forty, fifty, sixty, seventy, eighty, ninety. Ninety years old. *¡Noventa años!*

At breakfast Mamá says, "What is today, Cecilia?"

I say, "Secret day. Birthday day."

Mamá is cooking for the surprise party. I smell beans bubbling on the stove. Mamá is cutting fruit, pineapple, watermelon, mangoes. I sit in the backyard and watch Chica chase butterflies. I hear bees bzzzzzzz.

I draw pictures in the sand with a stick. I draw a picture of Tía, my aunt. I say, "Chica, what will we give Tía?"

Chica and I walk around the front yard and the backyard looking for a good present. We walk around the house. We look in Mamá's room. We look in my closet and drawers.

I say, "Chica, shall we give her my little pots, my piggy bank, my tin fish, my dancing puppet?"

I say, "Mamá, can Chica and I use this basket?"
Mamá asks, "Why, Cecilia?"

"It's a surprise for the surprise party," I answer.

Chica jumps into the basket. "No," I say. "Not you,
silly cat. This is a birthday basket for Tía."

I put a book at the bottom of the basket.

When Tía comes to our house, she reads it to me.
It's our favorite book. I sit close to her on the
sofa. I smell her perfume. Sometimes Chica tries
to read with us. She sits on the book. I say, "Silly
cat. Books are not for sitting."

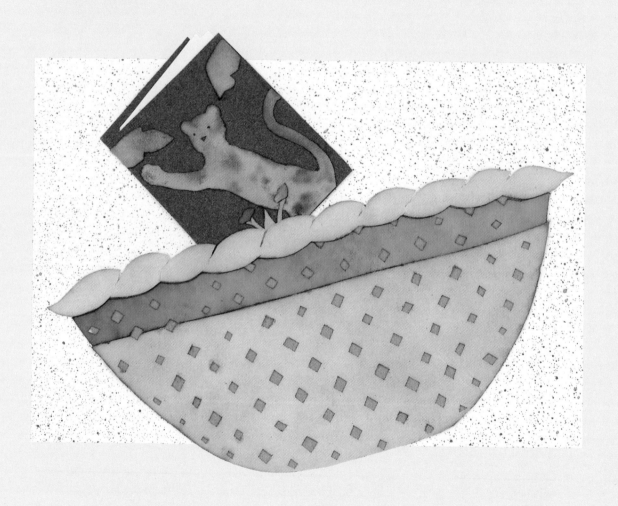

I put Tía's favorite mixing bowl on the book in the basket.

Tía and I like to make *bizcochos,* sugary Mexican cookies for the family.

Tía says, "Cecilia, help me stir the cookie dough." She says, "Cecilia, help me roll the cookie dough."

When we take the warm cookies from the oven, Tía says, "Cecilia, you are a very good cook."

I put a flowerpot in the mixing bowl on the book
in the basket.

Tía and I like to grow flowers for the kitchen
window. Chica likes to put her face in the flowers.
"Silly cat," I say.

I put a teacup in the flowerpot that is in the mixing bowl on the book in the basket.

When I'm sick, my aunt makes me hot mint tea, *hierbabuena.* She brings it to me in bed. She brings me a cookie too.

I put a red ball in the teacup that is in the
flowerpot in the mixing bowl on the book in the
basket.

On warm days Tía sits outside and throws me the
ball. She says, "Cecilia, when I was a little girl in
Mexico, my sisters and I played ball. We all wore
long dresses and had long braids."

Chica and I go outside. I pick flowers to decorate
Tía's basket. On summer days when I am
swinging high up to the sky, Tía collects flowers
for my room.

Mamá calls, "Cecilia, where are you?"

Chica and I run and hide our surprise.

I say, "Mamá, can you find the birthday basket for Tía?"

Mamá looks under the table. She looks in the refrigerator. She looks under my bed. She asks, "Chica, where is the birthday basket?"

Chica rubs against my closet door. Mamá and I laugh. I show her my surprise.

After my nap, Mamá and I fill a *piñata* with candy. We fill the living room with balloons. I hum, "MMMMM," a little work song like Tía hums when she sets the table or makes my bed. I help Mamá set the table with flowers and tiny cakes.

"Here come the musicians," says Mamá. I open the front door. Our family and friends begin to arrive too.

I curl Chica into my arms. Then Mamá says, "Sshh, here comes Tía."

I rush to open the front door. "Tía! Tía!" I say.

She hugs me and says, "Cecilia, *qué pasa,* what is this?"

"SURPRISE!" we all shout. "¡*Feliz cumpleaños!*
Happy birthday!" The musicians begin to play
their guitars and violins.

"Tía! Tía!" I say. "It's secret day, birthday day! It's your ninetieth birthday surprise party!" Tía and I start to laugh.

I give her the birthday basket. Everyone gets
close to see what's inside. Slowly Tía smells the
flowers. She looks at me and smiles.

Then she takes the red ball out of the teacup and
the teacup out of the flowerpot. She pretends to
take a sip of tea, and we all laugh.

Carefully, Tía takes the flowerpot out of the bowl and the bowl off of the book. She doesn't say a word. She just stops and looks at me. Then she takes our favorite book out of the basket.

And guess who jumps into the basket?
(Turn the page.)

Chica.

Everyone laughs.

Then the music starts and my aunt surprises me.
She takes my hands in hers. Without her cane,
she starts to dance with me.

Meet Cecily Lang

Cecily Lang says that watching people helps her be a better artist. She says, "I always peek at people and see how they're feeling by looking at their mouths and their cheeks. I look at their smiles and their frowns."

First, Ms. Lang draws pictures on regular paper. Next, she traces each part of the picture on a special piece of paper and cuts each piece with a sharp knife. Then, she dyes each piece of paper the color she wants. She puts the pieces together like a jigsaw puzzle and holds them together with tape. Then, she glues all the pieces together. Last, she colors the pieces lightly with a pencil.

MOLLY AND EMMETT

BY MARYLIN HAFNER

IT'S A BIG STORM, EM.

WOW! THAT WAS REALLY LOUD!

IT'S ONLY THUNDER UP IN THE CLOUDS, EMMETT...

BUT I DON'T LIKE IT EITHER, WHEN I'M ALL BY MYSELF.

YOU O.K., MOLLY?

I AM NOW, EM!

202

two friends

lydia and shirley have

two pierced ears and

two bare ones

five pigtails

two pairs of sneakers

two berets

two smiles

one necklace

one bracelet

lots of stripes and

one good friendship

Nikki Giovanni

Meet

Colleen Stanley Bare

Colleen Stanley Bare has taken pictures of many animals. One day she noticed how many kinds of guinea pigs there are. So she decided to write *Guinea Pigs Don't Read Books.*

Children often ask Ms. Bare, "How do you get a guinea pig?" She tells them, "Lots of pet shops have guinea pigs or you can look in newspapers under 'Pets' and find them advertised for sale."

Ms. Bare says that when she writes she has to pick out the very best words to use. "Each word in this book was crossed out and changed many times. I go over and over the words in my books until I like the way they sound."

Guinea Pigs Don't Read Books

by Colleen Stanley Bare

Guinea pigs don't read books,
count numbers, run computers,

play checkers, or watch TV,

but there are other things they do.

They chew, and chew, and chew.
Foods like apples, celery, carrots,
and if you don't watch out,
they'll chew your toys.

Guinea pigs see well
and stare at you.

They hear well
and listen.

They smell well
and sniff and sniff.

Guinea pigs make sounds.
They growl, grunt, gurgle,
purr, squeal, whistle,
and squeak, squeak, squeak.

Guinea pigs don't wear hats,
but they do wear fur coats.

Short, soft smooth ones

rough, bristly ones

long, silky ones.

Their coats come in many colors.

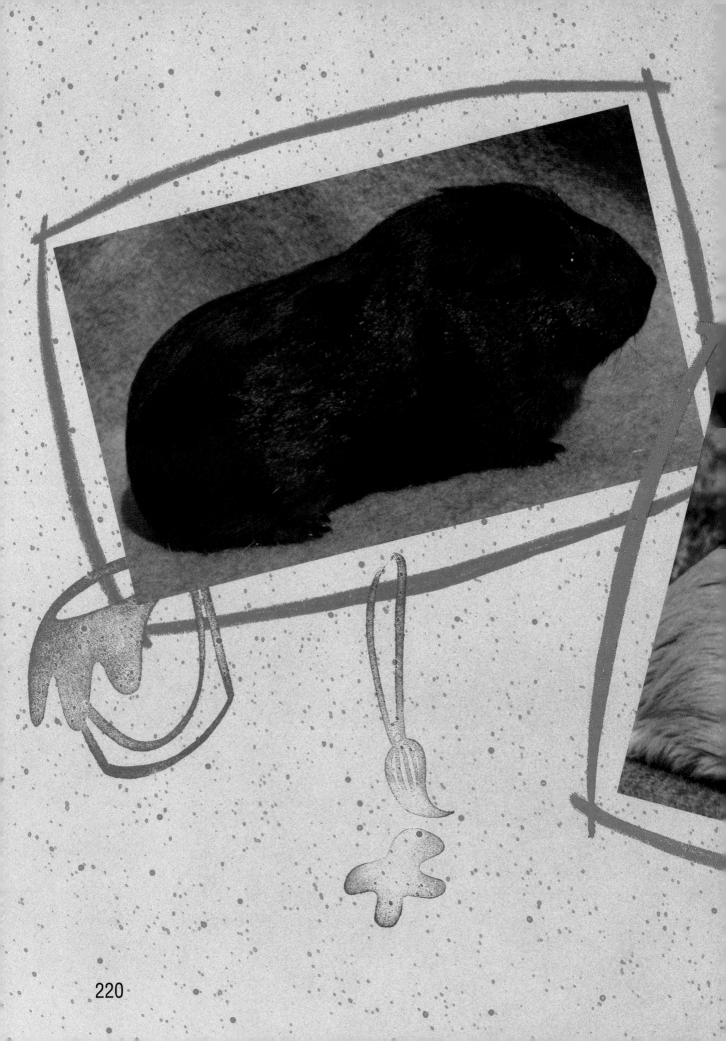

Blue, beige, cream,
red, orange, lilac,
chocolate, white, black.

And in mixtures of colors.

Guinea pigs aren't pigs.
They don't eat like pigs,
walk like pigs, sound like pigs.

Even baby guinea pigs
don't look like baby pigs.

Guinea pigs like to be held and hugged.
They are gentle and calm and lovable.

Guinea pigs may not read books,
but they can be your friends.

As the sun came up, a ball of red,

I followed my friend wherever he led.

He thought his fast horse would leave me behind,

But I rode a dragon as swift as the wind!

from **The Chinese Mother Goose**

MEET
EZRA JACK KEATS

Ezra Jack Keats made the pictures in *A Letter to Amy* by painting over pieces of paper that he cut, tore, and pasted down.

Mr. Keats got the idea for Peter from some pictures of a child that he cut out of a newspaper. He had these pictures for 22 years before he made the first book with Peter in it. Other books by Ezra Jack Keats about Peter include *The Snowy Day*, *Whistle for Willie*, and *Peter's Chair*.

EZRA JACK KEATS

It is this Saturday at 2

A
LETTER
TO AMY

"I'm writing a letter to Amy.

I'm inviting her to my party," Peter announced.

"Why don't you just ask her? You didn't write

to anyone else," said his mother.

Peter stared at the sheet of paper for a while and said,

"We-e-el-l, this way it's sort of special."

He folded the letter quite a few times,
put it in the envelope, and sealed it.
"Now I'll mail it," he said.
"What did you write?" his mother asked.
WILL YOU PLEASE COME
TO MY BIRTHDAY PARTY. PETER.
"You should tell her when to come."
So he wrote on the back of the envelope:
IT IS THIS SATURDAY AT 2.
"Now I'll mail it."
"Put on a stamp."
He did, and started to leave.
"Wear your raincoat. It looks like rain."
He put it on and said, "It looks like rain.
You'd better stay in, Willie,"
and ran out to mail his letter.

Walking to the mailbox, Peter looked at the sky.
Dark clouds raced across it like wild horses.
He glanced up at Amy's window. She wasn't there.
Only Pepe, her parrot, sat peering down.
"Willie! Didn't I tell you to stay home?"

Peter thought, What will the boys say
when they see a girl at my party?
Suddenly there was a flash of lightning
and a roar of thunder!
A strong wind blew the letter out of his hand!

Peter chased the letter.
He tried to stop it with his foot, but it blew away.

Then it flew high into the air—

and landed, skipping across a hopscotch game.

The letter blew this way and that.
Peter chased it this way and that.
He couldn't catch it.

Big drops of rain began to fall.
Just then someone turned the corner.
It was Amy! She waved to him.
The letter flew right toward her.

She mustn't see it, or the surprise will be spoiled!
They both ran for the letter.

In his great hurry, Peter bumped into Amy.
He caught the letter before she could see it was for her.

Quickly he stuffed the letter into the mailbox.
He looked for Amy, but she had run off crying.

Now she'll never come to my party, thought Peter.
He saw his reflection in the street.
It looked all mixed up.

When Peter got back to his house, his mother asked, "Did you mail your letter?"

"Yes," he said sadly.

Saturday came at last.
Everybody arrived but Amy.

"Shall I bring the cake out now?" his mother asked Peter.

"Let's wait a little," said Peter.

"Now! Bring it out now!" chanted the boys.

"All right," said Peter slowly, "bring it out now."

Just then the door opened.
In walked Amy with her parrot!
"A girl—ugh!" said Eddie.

"Happy Birthday, Peter!" said Amy.
"HAAPPY BIRRRTHDAY, PEEETERRR!"
  repeated the parrot.

Peter's mother brought in the cake she had baked and lit the candles. Everyone sang.

"Make a wish!" cried Amy.

"Wish for a truck full of ice cream!" shouted Eddie.

"A store full of candy and no stomach-ache!"

But Peter made his own wish,
and blew out all the candles at once.

Surprise Letter

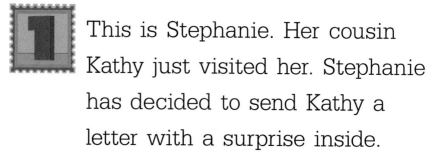

This is Stephanie. Her cousin Kathy just visited her. Stephanie has decided to send Kathy a letter with a surprise inside.

2 Stephanie took the letter to the post office. She put it into the mail slot. Bye-bye, letter!

3 In the post office the letters are dumped onto a moving belt. People and machines sort the mail. Every letter has a place to go.

4 All the mail gets stacked, bundled, and put in sacks. The sacks of mail are driven outside to the loading dock.

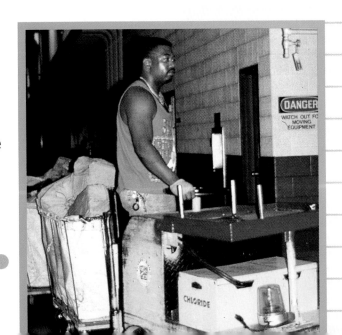

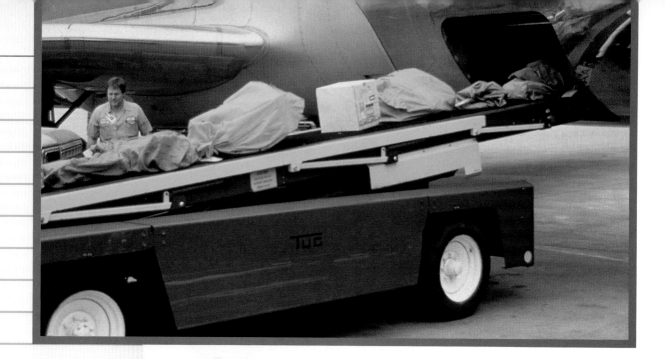

 Kathy's town is far away. All
the letters going there will ride
in a plane.

 The mail carrier in Kathy's
neighborhood brings the letter to
Kathy's house.

What's inside
the letter?

 Kathy opens
the letter.
"Look what
I got in the
mail," she says.
"It's a picture
of Stephanie
and me!"

266

Friends

On Saturday,
No matter the weather,
The three of us
Will get together
And play whatever
We want to play,
And wish all week
Was Saturday.

D.J. Allan

READING RESOURCES

CONTENTS

Greetings from Washington D.C.

ar Families
ahn's Class

h

inea
Pigs

Snakes

A house

WHAT?
THDAY PARTY!
PLEASE COME
Myra L.
May 16, 3 o'cl
5 Oak Stree
55 - 614

Mr. Jason Peck
P.O. Box 005
Ithaca College
Ithaca, NY 14850-0000

Mr. Antonio
Vice Pres
Texas Al
35 Mesa
Austin, TX

U.S.MAIL

PARK

ADDRESSES

Return Address

Maria Rosales
Calle San José 159
San Juan, Puerto Rico 00901-0000

Postage

$2.39

FRAGILE

Mailing Address

Mrs. Sara Stein
119 Oak Drive
Columbus, Ohio 43221-0000

FRAGILE

ADDRESSES

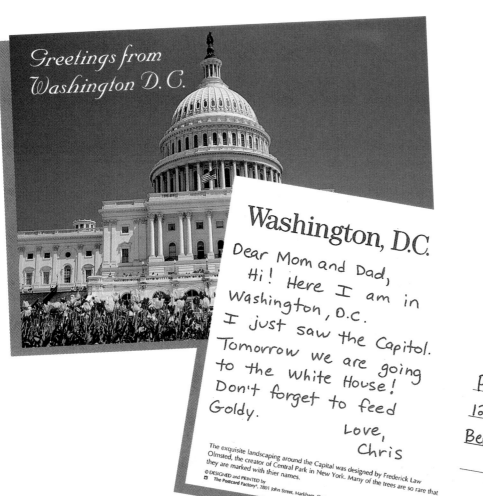

Greetings from Washington D.C.

Washington, D.C.

Dear Mom and Dad,
 Hi! Here I am in
Washington, D.C.
I just saw the Capitol.
Tomorrow we are going
to the white House!
Don't forget to feed
Goldy.
 Love,
 Chris

The exquisite landscaping around the Capital was designed by Frederick Law
Olmsted, the creator of Central Park in New York. Many of the trees are so rare that
they are marked with thier names.
© DESIGNED and PRINTED by
☒ The Postcard Factory®, 2801 John Street, Markham, Onatario L3R 1B4 (905) 477-9901

Printed in Canada

Photo by: R. Kord / H. Armstrong Roberts / Comstock
Ref: WDC-50

Paul and Lani Yee
1247 Oxford Street
Berkeley, CA 94707-0000

Mr. Jason Peck
P.O. Box 005
Ithaca College
Ithaca, NY 14850-0000

Mr. Antonio Velez
Vice President, Human Resources
Texas Alive! Magazine
35 Mesa Drive
Austin, TX 78767-0000

DICTIONARY

bill
A **bill** is the hard part of a bird's mouth. **Bill** is another word for **beak**. ▲ **bills**.

biography
A **biography** is a true story of someone's life written by another person. ▲ **biographies**.

bird
A **bird** is an animal with wings. **Birds** are covered with feathers and have two legs. Most **birds** can fly. **Birds** lay eggs. Chickens, robins, and penguins are **birds**. ▲ **birds**.

We sang "Happy Birthday" to Tommy on his **birthday**.

birthday
Your **birthday** is the day and month when you were born. Keith and I have the same **birthday**. ▲ **birthdays**.

bite
1. **Bite** means to cut something with the teeth. The dog tried to **bite** the stick I threw her. Jesse **bit** into the apple.
▲ **bit, bitten** or **bit, biting**.
2. A **bite** is a piece you get when you **bite**. Jack took a **bite** of the banana. ▲ **bites**.

black
Black is a very dark color. These letters are **black**. The opposite of **black** is **white**.

blame
Blame means to say that a person has done something wrong or bad. Mother **blamed** me for letting the bird out of its cage.
▲ **blamed, blaming**.

Who took a **bite** out of Will's sandwich?

39

DICTIONARY

celebrate
When you **celebrate** something, you show that it is important in a special way. Our town **celebrated** the Fourth of July with a parade and fireworks. ▲ **celebrated, celebrating.**

Our family **celebrated** Grandma and Grandpa's 50th wedding anniversary.

center
Center means middle. Cassie stood in the **center** of the circle for the game. We put the flowers in the **center** of the table. ▲ **centers.**

cereal
Cereal is a food often made from wheat, corn, or rice. We like **cereal** for breakfast. ▲ **cereals.**

certain
Certain means that you are very sure about something. Are you **certain** that you closed the door?

chain
A **chain** is a row of rings that are joined together. Margaret wore a heart on a **chain** around her neck. ▲ **chains.**

chair
A **chair** is a piece of furniture with four legs and a back. People sit on **chairs.** ▲ **chairs.**

Meg is using a **chain** to keep her bike safe.

65

DIRECTIONS

ANIMAL MASKS

Use your imagination to make an animal mask. Here's what you will need:

- a large paper bag
- scissors
- glue
- construction paper
- crayons, felt-tip pens, or magic markers

HERE'S WHAT TO DO:

1.
First, put the paper bag over your head and have a friend make marks for eye holes and arm holes.

2.
Take the bag off. Then, cut holes for your eyes and arms.

3.
Now draw and color eyes and mouth.

4.
Next, make ears, nose, and other parts from construction paper. Glue them to the paper bag.

5.
Finally, you may want to add other things — like feathers or straws.

DIRECTIONS

CLAY DOUGH

Clay dough is soft. You can use it to make a red strawberry, a green donkey, or almost anything you can imagine. You can buy clay dough, but you can also make it. Here is what you need:

- flour
- water
- salt

- vegetable oil
- a large bowl
- measuring cups
- food coloring

DIRECTIONS FOR MAKING CLAY DOUGH

1. Mix 1 1/2 cups of flour and 1/2 cup of salt in a bowl.

2. Stir in 1/2 cup of water and 1/2 cup of vegetable oil. Then add food coloring.

3. Squeeze the mixture with your hands for 3 or 4 minutes. Wet your hands if the mixture doesn't hold together. When it feels like clay, it is ready to use.

Now you're ready to play with clay dough. You can roll it, pat it, flatten it, pinch it, and mold it however you want.

DIRECTIONS

WHAT?

A BIRTHDAY PARTY!
PLEASE COME

WHO: Myra L.

WHEN: May 16, 3 o'clock

WHERE: 15 Oak Street

Please reply 555-6145

To get to my house from School:

1. Leave by front door, turn right, go to Holly.
2. Turn left at Holly.
3. Go to Oak, cross Oak.
4. Turn right, go to Elm, cross Elm.

My house is the second from the corner.

MY HOUSE

ELM ROAD

OAK STREET

PARK

HOLLY ROAD

PINE STREET

15

front SCHOOL

GRAPHS

Pets in Our Families
by Ms. Kahn's Class

Dogs

Cats

Fish

Guinea Pigs

Snakes

⌂ = 1 household with pet

MAPS

The Playground

KEY

- Monkey Bars
- Slide
- Bike Rack
- Sandbox
- Sprinklers
- Restrooms
- Seesaws
- Swings
- Water Fountain

SCHEDULES

Angel's and Artie's Schedule			
	Take Out Recycling	Feed Dog	Water Plants
Monday	Angel	Artie	Angel
Tuesday		Angel	
Wednesday		Artie	
Thursday	Artie	Angel	Artie
Friday		Artie	
Saturday		Angel	
Sunday		Artie	Angel

GLOS

This glossary can help you to find out the meanings of words in this book that you may not know.

SARY

The words are listed in
alphabetical order. Guide words
at the top of each page tell you the
first and last words on the page.

against

To be **against** something means to be touching or toward something. Rosa left her bicycle **against** the tree.

apple

An **apple** is a round fruit with red, yellow, or green skin. **Apples** grow on trees. ▲ **apples.**

apples

attic

An **attic** is the space or room below the roof of a house. **Attics** are sometimes used as places to keep old clothes or furniture. ▲ **attics.**

B b

bananas

banana

A **banana** is a long fruit with yellow or red skin. **Bananas** grow in bunches on big plants that look like trees.
▲ **bananas.**

basket

A **basket** is something made of straw or wood that is used to hold things. We put all the food for the picnic into a big **basket.** ▲ **baskets.**

before

Before means ahead of in time or place. We will be home from school **before** lunch because the teachers have a meeting in the afternoon.

birthday

Your **birthday** is the day and month when you were born. Keith and I have the same **birthday.** ▲ **birthdays.**

blame

Blame means the cause of something wrong or bad. Ed took the **blame** for letting the dog get mud on the floor.

board

A **board** is a long, flat piece of wood. **Boards** are used to build houses and other things. ▲ **boards.**

breakfast

Breakfast is the first meal of the day. I like fried eggs, toast, and juice for **breakfast.** ▲ **breakfasts.**

breakfast

bristly

Bristly means full of short, stiff hair. The hair on the back of my neck feels **bristly.**

Cc

capture

Capture means to catch and hold a person, animal, or thing. The man will **capture** the butterfly and then let it go. ▲ **captured, capturing.**

carrot

A **carrot** is a long, orange vegetable that grows in the ground. My rabbit ate the **carrot** right out of my hand. ▲ **carrots.**

carrot

chew

Chew means to cut something with the teeth. Our new puppy likes to **chew** shoes. ▲ **chewed, chewing.**

climb

Climb means to move up something using your hands and feet. Mom had to **climb** a ladder to get the kite out of the tree. ▲ **climbed, climbing.**

collect

Collect means to gather things together. I like to **collect** different kinds of rocks as a hobby. ▲ **collected, collecting.**

color

Red, blue, and yellow are the main **colors.** All other **colors** have some red, blue, or yellow in them. Orange is my favorite **color.** ▲ **colors.**

computer

A **computer** is a machine that can do many kinds of work very fast. My sister uses a **computer** to do her homework. ▲ **computers.**

crayons

crayon

A **crayon** is a wax stick that is used for writing and drawing. **Crayons** are made in many different colors. ▲ **crayons.**

crowd

A **crowd** is a large group of people in one place. The **crowd** waited for the game to start. ▲ **crowds.**

D d

donkey

A **donkey** is an animal that looks like a horse with longer ears. The **donkey** pulled the cart up the hill. ▲ **donkeys.**

donkey

E e

empty

When something is **empty,** there is nothing in it. After the puppy ate its food, its dish was **empty.**

G7

envelopes

envelope

An **envelope** is a flat wrapper or container used for mailing and holding letters. People mail letters and cards in **envelopes.** ▲ **envelopes.**

everyone

Everyone means all the people in a group. **Everyone** left the building during the fire drill.

favorite

Favorite means to be liked best. Christopher always wears his **favorite** cap.

finally

Finally means at the end. After riding for three hours in a bus, we **finally** reached our camp in the mountains.

flowers

flower

A **flower** is the part of a plant that makes seeds and usually has brightly colored petals. **Flowers** grow in many different colors. ▲ **flowers.**

fruit

A **fruit** is a part of a plant that holds the seeds and can usually be eaten. Apples, peaches, and oranges are kinds of **fruits.** ▲ **fruit** or **fruits.**

fur

Fur is the hair that covers an animal's body. Our dog's **fur** is white and black. ▲ **furs.**

G g

gifts

gift

A **gift** is something special that one person gives to another person. This book was a birthday **gift** from my cousin. ▲ **gifts.**

guess

To **guess** means to have an idea about something without knowing for sure if you are right. Ellen tried to **guess** who was behind her. ▲ **guessed, guessing.**

Hh

hard

When something is **hard** to do, it takes much effort or energy. This puzzle is very **hard** to do. ▲ **harder, hardest.**

Ii

invite

Invite means to ask someone to go somewhere. Alex gave Jill a card to **invite** her to his party. ▲ **invited, inviting.**

invite

Ll

ladder

A **ladder** is a set of steps that can be moved from one place to another. Mr. Fox used a **ladder** when he painted the top part of our house. ▲ **ladders.**

laugh

Laugh means to make sounds with your voice that show you think something is funny. Willie's jokes always make me **laugh.** ▲ **laughed, laughing.**

letter

A **letter** is a message that somebody writes on paper to send to somebody else. I got a **letter** in the mail today. ▲ **letters.**

ladder

Mm

machine

A **machine** is something we use to do work. Cranes are **machines** that lift heavy things. ▲ **machines.**

marble

A **marble** is a small, hard ball of glass used in games. Amy drew a big circle on the ground for a game of **marbles.** ▲ **marbles.**

marbles

music

When you sing, you are making **music.** Instruments, such as the piano and violin, also make **music.**

mystery

A **mystery** is something that is not known or that is hard to explain. The answer to that math problem was a **mystery** to Elena. ▲ **mysteries.**

Pp

package

A **package** is a box with something in it. We sent a **package** of treats to my sister at camp. ▲ **packages.**

paint

Paint is a liquid used to put color on things. **Paint** also means to put **paint** on something. This **paint** will dry very fast. Paul **painted** a picture of a farm. ▲ **paints, painted, painting.**

parrot

A **parrot** is a kind of bird. **Parrots** may have blue, green, red, or yellow feathers. ▲ **parrots.**

parrot

G13

party

A **party** is a lot of people who are having a good time together. We wore costumes to the surprise **party.**

▲ **parties.**

party

picture

A **picture** is something that you draw or paint. I have a **picture** of a boat on my wall. ▲ **pictures.**

plane

Plane is a short word for airplane. Serena likes to make model **planes.**
▲ **planes.**

plane

present

A **present** is something you give someone for a special reason. Each of the children brought a **present** to the party. ▲ **presents.**

quiet

Quiet means that there isn't any sound in a place. The house was so **quiet** you could hear the wind outside. ▲ **quieter, quietest.**

G15

Rr

reflection

A **reflection** is what you see when you look in a mirror or in very shiny things. He saw his **reflection** in the window. ▲ **reflections.**

reflection

remember

When we **remember** something, we think of it again, or we do not forget it. I will always **remember** when I got my puppy. ▲ **remembered, remembering.**

S s

secret

A **secret** is something that not many people know. The present I'm giving my mother for her birthday is my **secret.** ▲ **secrets.**

seesaw

A **seesaw** is a long board that two people sit on to make it go up and down. When one end of the **seesaw** is down, the other end is up. ▲ **seesaws.**

seesaw

share

Share means to give some of what you have to someone else. Roberto said he would **share** his cookies with us. ▲ **shared, sharing.**

shoe

A **shoe** is something that you wear on your foot. **Shoes** may be worn over socks. ▲ **shoes.**

smell

To **smell** means to be aware of an odor by using your nose. We could **smell** the turkey roasting in the oven. ▲ **smelled** or **smelt, smelling.**

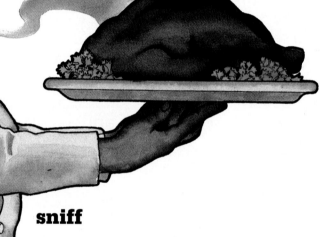

smell

sniff

When you **sniff,** you breathe in quickly through your nose. The kitten likes to **sniff** its food. ▲ **sniffed, sniffing.**

someone

Someone means a person, but you don't know which person. **Someone** left the door open.

special

When something is **special**, it is important and not like anything else. Your birthday is a **special** day.

spider

A **spider** is a kind of bug that has eight legs. A **spider** can spin a web.
▲ **spiders.**

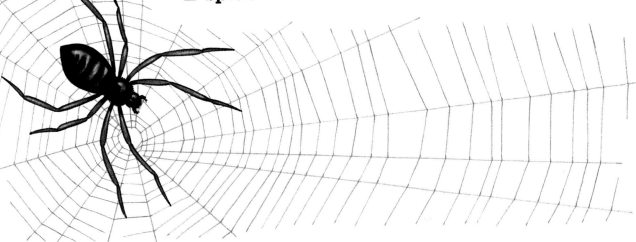

spider

stamp

A **stamp** is a small piece of paper that is put on a letter to mail it. You buy **stamps** at the post office. ▲ **stamps.**

store

A **store** is a place where you buy things. We went to the shoe **store,** and I got a new pair of shoes. ▲ **stores.**

storm

A **storm** is a strong wind with a lot of rain or snow. I woke up at night because of the **storm.** ▲ **storms.**

string

A **string** is a thin piece of rope. I fly my kite on a very long **string.** ▲ **strings.**

toy

A **toy** is a thing to play with. Dolls, kites, and balls are **toys.** ▲ **toys.**

toys

G20

W w

watch

Watch means to look at something carefully. The baby-sitter **watched** the children while they played. ▲ **watched, watching.**

wish

A **wish** is something that you want very much. Jesse made a **wish** for a new bicycle and then blew out the candles on the birthday cake. ▲ **wishes.**

wish

G21

ACKNOWLEDGMENTS

The publisher gratefully acknowledges permission to reprint the following copyrighted material:

"As the sun came up, a ball of red..." reprinted by permission of Philomel Books from CHINESE MOTHER GOOSE RHYMES selected & edited by Robert Wyndham, copyright © 1968 by Robert Wyndham.

"A Birthday Basket for Tía" from A BIRTHDAY BASKET FOR TÍA by Pat Mora. Illustrations by Cecily Lang. Text copyright © 1992 by Pat Mora. Illustrations copyright © 1992 by Cecily Lang. Reprinted with the permission of Simon & Schuster Books For Young Readers, Simon & Schuster Children's Publishing Division.

"By Myself" from HONEY, I LOVE by Eloise Greenfield. Illustrated by Diane and Leo Dillon. Text copyright © 1978 by Eloise Greenfield. Illustrations copyright © 1978 by Diane and Leo Dillon. Reprinted by permission of HarperCollins Publishers.

"Friends" by D. J. Allan. Reprinted by permission.

"Guinea Pigs Don't Read Books" from GUINEA PIGS DON'T READ BOOKS by Colleen Stanley Bare. Copyright © 1985 by Colleen Stanley Bare. Used by permission of Cobblehill Books, an affiliate of Dutton Children's Books, a division of Penguin USA, Inc.

"Hug O'War" by Shel Silverstein from WHERE THE SIDEWALK ENDS. Copyright (c) 1974 Evil Eye Music, Inc.

"Imaginary Zoo" by Ann Klein from CRAYOLA KIDS, February/March 1995 reprinted with permission of CRAYOLA KIDS™ magazine. Copyright © Meredith Corportation 1995. All rights reserved. Crayola® and Crayola Kids™ are trademarks of Binney & Smith Properties, Inc.

"In the Attic" from IN THE ATTIC by Hiawyn Oram, illustrated by Satoshi Kitamura. Text copyright © 1984 by Hiawyn Oram. Illustrations copyright © 1984 by Satoshi Kitamura. Reprinted by permission of Henry Holt and Co., Inc.

"Jimmy Lee Did It" Text and Art, JIMMY LEE DID IT by Pat Cummings. Text copyright © 1985 by Pat Cummings. By permission of Lothrop, Lee & Shepard Books, a division of William Morrow & Company, Inc.

"Julieta and Her Paintbox" by Carlos Pellicer Lopez, translated from JULIETA Y SU CAJA DECOLORES, copyright Editorial Patria, S.A. Reprinted by permission.

"Just a Little Bit" by Anne Tompert, illustrated by Lynn Munsinger, copyright © 1993 by Ann Tompert and Lynn Munsinger, published by Houghton Mifflin & Company. Reprinted by permission.

"A Letter to Amy" is the entire work of A LETTER TO AMY by Ezra Jack Keats. Copyright © 1968 by Ezra Jack Keats. Reprinted by permission of HarperCollins Publishers.

"Like a Summer Bird" by Aileen Fisher. Reprinted by permission.

"Molly and Emmett" by Marylin Hafner, from LADYBUG, September 1992. Copyright © 1992 by Marylin Hafner, published by Carus Publishing Company. Reprinted by permission.

Entire text, art, and cover of "New Shoes for Silvia" by Johanna Hurwitz. Illustrated by Jerry Pinkney. Text copyright (c) 1993 by Johanna Hurwitz. Illustrations copyright (c) 1993 by Jerry Pinkney. By permission of Morrow Junior Books, a division of William Morrow and Company, Inc.

"Pretending" by Bobbi Katz from UPSIDE DOWN AND INSIDE OUT: POEMS FOR ALL YOUR POCKETS by Bobbi Katz. Copyright © 1973 by Bobbi Katz. Used by permission of the author who controls all rights.

"Square as a House" by Karla Kuskin. Reprinted by permission.

Photographs from "Surprise Letter" from HERE COMES THE MAIL by Gloria Skurzynski. Copyright (c) 1992 by Gloria Skurzynski. Reprinted with permission of Simon & Schuster Books for Young Readers, Simon and Schuster Children's Publishing Division.

"Surprise Letter" text only from SESAME STREET MAGAZINE, April 1995, Copyright © 1995. Reprinted by permission.

"two friends" from SPIN A SOFT BLACK SONG by Nikki Giovanni, Copyright © 1971, 1985 by Nikki Giovanni. Used by arrangement with Farrar, Straus and Giroux, Inc.

READING RESOURCES

Dictionary: Excerpt from MACMILLAN PRIMARY DICTIONARY, copyright © 1991 by Macmillan/McGraw-Hill School Publishing Company. Reprinted by permission of Macmillan/McGraw-Hill School Publishing Company.

COVER DESIGN: Carbone Smolan Associates
COVER ILLUSTRATION: Brad Sneed (front - dog), Wallace Keller (front - girl in chair and back)

DESIGN CREDITS
Carbone Smolan Associates, front matter and unit openers
Bill Smith Studio, 72-73, 132-133, 202-203, 263-265
Function Thru Form, Inc., 268-271, 277-279
Sheldon Cotler + Associates Editorial Group, 170-201, 232-261
Notovitz Design Inc., 272-276

ILLUSTRATION CREDITS
Unit 1: Wallace Keller, 8-9; P. D. Cooper, 38-39; Susan Huls, 40-71 (typography); Bernard Adnet, 72-73 (shadows); Jo Lynn Alcorn, 72-73 (title and border); Bernard Adnet, 132-133. **Unit 2:** Brad Sneed, 136-137; April Blair-Stewart, 202-203 (borders); Mary Anne Lloyd 206-229 (stamp art); Jill Karla Schwartz, 230-231; Bill Frampton, 262-265; Lisa Henderling, 267. **Reading Resources:** George Poladian, 274-275; Felicia Telsey, 277; Patrick Merrill, 278. **Glossary:** Will and Cory Nelson, G2, G5-G9, G11, G13; Bob Pepper, G10, G14, G17, G18, G21.

PHOTOGRAPHY CREDITS
All photographs are by the Macmillan/McGraw-Hill School Division (MMSD) except as noted below.

1: Craig Tuttle/Stock Market. 4: b. Rick Gayle/The Stock Market. 8: t.l. Monica Stevenson for MMSD. 12: l. Rick Gayle/The Stock Market. 15: t. Superstock. 16: m. Paul Damien/Tony Stone Images, Inc. **Unit 1** 38-39: Francis Clark Westfield/MMSD. 74-75: Christoph Burki/Tony Stone International. 104: t. Amanda Smith/William Morrow & Co.; b. Alan Orling/William Morrow & Co. 104-105: Ken Cavanagh. **Unit 2** 138: t. Ann Tompert. 138: b. Houghton Mifflin Co. 263-265: Gloria Skurzynski/Simon & Schuster Children's Publishing Division. 266-267: Francis Westfield for MMSD. **Unit 7** 1: l. Superstock; Inga Spence/Tom Stack & Associates; Superstock; Comstock; Jack Van Antwerp/Stock Market. 271: Everett Johnson/Tony Stone Images.

The Test-Taker's
HANDBOOK

How to Use These Pages

Sometimes, a test can make you worry. These pages will help you feel better about taking tests.

You will learn new things to use when you take a test. You will also learn how to use what you know. This can help make it easier to take a test. You can make up rhymes or other games to help you remember what to do.

These pages will help with tests that your teacher gives you. It will also help you with special tests.

Before you take a test, read these pages again. Each time you do, you will learn more. That will help you be a better test-taker.

Hints for Taking Tests

Do you think that Sammy Sosa practices before a big baseball game? You bet!

Before you take a test, you can practice, too.

Think about these hints and tips. Practice as many as you can.

It Takes Practice

Practice to get in shape before a test.

FIND OUT

★ Ask what will be on the test.

★ Will it be a book test?

★ Will it be a special test?

LOOK BACK

★ Look at old tests. Look at old work papers.

★ Look at what you did right.

★ Know what you did not do right.

The flower is **lovely.**

○ smelly

○ big

○ pretty

○ old

What happened last in the story?

○ Nancy opened her eyes.

○ Dave and Nancy played catch.

○ Mom called to Dave.

○ Nancy fell asleep at last.

What is the main idea of the story?

○ Clowns work hard.

○ Clowns wear funny hats.

○ The circus is fun!

○ Lions are big and loud.

Show What You Know

Do you worry about taking a test? That's OK — everyone worries about it sometimes.

Say to yourself, "I can do this!"

Think about work you have done before. Think about what you know about reading.

Oh, I remember doing one like this for homework.

TRY:

★ rereading

★ looking for clue words

★ using other words in the sentence

★ thinking about words that have the same meaning as a new word

Hmm, I better check this answer again.

Double Check

- When you finish a question, ask yourself:

  ☐ Does my answer make sense?

  ☐ Did I answer the question?

Be Careful

I can't answer this. I don't have enough information.

My answer is not one of the choices.

This answer doesn't make sense, but it is one of the choices so it must be right.

The right answers have been first and third, so all the right answers must be first and third.

You know better!

These hints can help you make fewer mistakes:

- Look for clue words in the question.

- Look for clue words in the answer.

- Use time-order words to help you.

- Watch for words that have more than one meaning. Use the other words in the sentence to help you.

Preparing for Tests

A multiple-choice test can be an easy test to take. Why? Because you know the right answer is right there. You just have to figure out which one it is.

O blue crayons
O black pens
O red paint
● green markers

Fill in only one circle for each question.

Fill in the correct circle all the way.

Jones Beach is one of the best beaches in the world. The sand is smooth and clean. There are places to picnic and places to listen to music. The waves can be very rough. Swimmers sometimes have to be careful. But the ocean is always beautiful and the beach is fun.

Find and reread the word in the story.

1 The word <u>rough</u> in this story means
O bumpy
O dangerous
O wet
O smooth

Sometimes answers don't make sense. Forget those choices right away.

2 What is the sand like at Jones Beach?
O scratchy
O red
O smooth and clean
O hard and hot

Practicing Reading Tests

Directions

Read the passage. Then read each question about the story. Choose the best answer to each question. Mark the space for the answer you have chosen.

Look for key words to help you find the answer.

Mario and his family are taking a trip. They are going to California. It is far from Denver, but they will have fun on the way. First, Mario's mom will let them listen to music. Mario and his sister will sing along. Later, they will stop for a picnic lunch in a pretty meadow. The next day, the whole family will play counting games. Mario thinks the best part of the trip might be riding in the car!

Use other words in the sentence to help you learn the meaning of a new word.

1 Where does the trip start?

   ○ California

   ○ the park

   ○ the car

   ○ Denver

2 What does meadow mean in this passage?

   ○ lunch

   ○ a pretty place to sit and eat

   ○ a delicious picnic

   ○ a long car trip

Practicing Reading Tests

Directions

Read the letter. Then read each question about the letter. Choose the best answer to each question. Mark the space for the answer you have chosen.

Try to match words in the passage with words in the question. Look for time-order words.

Dear Aunt Paula,

I went to the circus today. First, we saw horses and riders. They were beautiful. Next the acrobats came out and did their jumping and tumbling tricks. That was exciting! At last, the big circus parade closed the show.

Maybe next year, you will be able to come with us. I think you will have a good time, too.

Your nephew,

Danny

3 What happened last at the circus?

- ○ The horses and riders came out.
- ○ Danny saw lions and tigers.
- ○ Danny saw the circus parade.
- ○ The acrobats jumped and tumbled.

4 Who wrote the letter?

- ○ Danny
- ○ Aunt Paula
- ○ acrobats
- ○ horseback riders

Use special clues and what you know about friendly letters to help you find the answer.